A PORTRAIT OF
BIRMINGHAM

VAN GREAVES

HALSGROVE

First published in Great Britain in 2004

Frontispiece photograph: **City Skyline and Bartley Green Reservoir**

British Library Cataloguing-in-Publication Data
A CIP record for this title is available from the British Library

ISBN 1 84114 375 8

HALSGROVE
Halsgrove House
Lower Moor Way
Tiverton, Devon EX16 6SS
Tel: 01884 243242
Fax: 01884 243325
email: sales@halsgrove.com
website: www.halsgrove.com

Printed and bound by D'Auria Industrie Grafiche Spa, Italy

INTRODUCTION

Birmingham is the city of invention and re-invention. Although recorded from the time of Domesday, its real significance to Britain and the world came over the last two hundred years, when it grew rapidly in stature to become Britain's second city.

Somehow, it gets away with major alteration, retaining high Victoriana with modern building designs, both traditional and futuristic. People aged over fifty years can vouch from memory many places, buildings and roads which have disappeared or altered out of all recognition. There have been three Bull Rings since the last war, the latest, a swish twenty-first century statement to modern shopping.

Once 'the city of a thousand trades,' Birmingham is now more of a commercial, tourism and shopping magnet. This is seen particularly where the network of canals – more it is said than in Venice – have been resurrected from former decline and are now surrounded by elegant café bars, shops, civic facilities, walkways and pubs.

From the city centre, motorways and trunk roads fan out in all directions feeding the international airport and National Exhibition Centre and many former villages, such as Moseley, Yardley, Northfield, King's Norton, King's Heath, and Harborne. These tranquil communities have now become fashionable suburbs, immersed within the city boundary.

The impressive city skyline, decked with a foreground profusion of trees, can be seen from boundary hills such as the Lickeys, Clent and Barr Beacon, Many more trees are to be found in the over 150 public parks and open spaces evenly spread across the city. Noteworthy are the (formal) Cannon Hill Park, and the (wild) Woodgate Valley Country Park.

A photographic book of Birmingham must obviously be selective, but I have tried to give an overall 'feel' to what is nowadays a vibrant city. The photographs range from straight record shots to unusual or design angles, always seeking strongly visual results within the ever-present limits of time, light and weather.

Van Greaves, 2004

Christmas at Harrods, Corporation Street
It was worth the upward view for the interesting angles and lighting.

Birmingham Eye, Centenary Square
The large Ferris wheel was a temporary seasonal landmark and ride. It may be gone for the present, but it might well be back.

Iron Man, Victoria Square
The controversial leaning figure by Anthony Gormley
raises a few questions – perhaps about his sobriety?

Cadbury's, Bournville, in the autumn

**Serbian Orthodox Church,
Griffins Brook Lane, Selly Oak**
Architecture which reflects
Eastern European design.

**Spire and Blossom,
St Nicholas Church, King's Norton**
This medieval church is
of fifteenth-century design
and is a focal point of the
former village, one of many
which have now been
swallowed up by the city.

Wildfowl on Witton Lakes

Grove Park, Harborne
Spring meets winter as crocuses
struggle against a cold snap.

11

Alexander Stadium, Perry Park

The low angle on the curves of the track lanes lend dynamism to this photograph of Birmingham's major athletics stadium.

West Bromwich Albion v Bradford City
You could throw a stone from the city boundary into The Hawthorns, the home ground of West Bromwich Albion football club, and it is included for the sake of its many Birmingham-based supporters (including the photographer).

Birmingham City v Liverpool
Robbie Savage flights in an attacking cross in vain, as Liverpool cruise to a comfortable 3-0 victory
at St Andrews, the home ground of Birmingham City FC.

Aston Villa v Newcastle, Villa Park
The size of the players gives scale to this part of the grand structure which is Villa Park.

Gertrude Terrace, Birmingham 18
This is a fine example of a restored Victorian courtyard terrace.

Gertrude Place, Birmingham 18
Another late-Victorian terraced facade.

**Springfield Library and
Canterbury Tower, Ladywood**
A juxtaposition of architectural
contrasts in this carefully-composed
picture, which was only possible
on a well-lit summer morning.

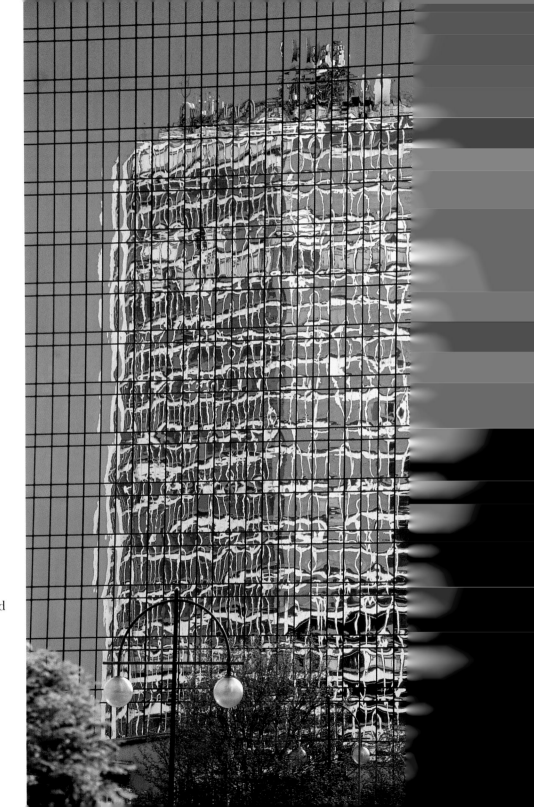

**Alpha Tower reflected in
the Hyatt Hotel, Broad Street**
An interesting composition provided
by modern architectural design.

Brindley Place
This is one of the numerous squares
in the 'new' Birmingham, centred
around the canal basins.

Symphony Court and the National Indoor Arena

21

Apartments and tree, Symphony Court
The last maple leaves on the tree contrast nicely
with the modern apartments behind.

Sherbourne Wharf
The boats and the building make for an interesting pattern.

Christmas in the Bull Ring

Spring Show, Cannon Hill Park
This is a popular park, particularly
when it is adorned by its
springtime show of tulips.

Millstream Way and Sarehole Mill, Moseley
This walk goes through a green corridor in one of J.R.R. Tolkien's (author of *Lord of the Rings*) local haunts.

Sarehole Mill, Moseley
There has been a mill here for grinding corn since the sixteenth century.

Yardley Village
This shows the older part of Yardley, near the fifteenth-century church of St Edburgha.

Stormlight, St Edburgha's Church, Yardley
This view belies the fact that Yardley is now a city suburb, and shows its rural origins.

**Clock Tower, Aston Cross,
and HP Sauce Factory**
The clock is one of several similar
structures, now over 100 years old.
The product made in the factory
is a household name. Getting two
quite dissimilar subjects into one
photograph seemed to work here.

Longbridge: the older part of the factory

A surviving industrial institution synonymous with Birmingham, seen with an up-to-date sporting version of a Rover car.

'Hancock', Priory Ringway
The laconic comedian, though born in Hall Green, Birmingham, spent only a brief part of his life there.

The Bull of the Bull Ring
This dynamic new statue guards the entrance
to the new Bull Ring Shopping Centre.

Highbury Hall, Moseley
The home of one of Birmingham's most famous city fathers, Joseph Chamberlain, stands in its own grounds.

Bells Farm, Druids Heath
Once a genuine farm out in the countryside, the historic Bells Farm, a listed building and museum,
is nowadays in the company of 1960s high-rise blocks of flats and a housing estate.

Moseley Baths
These premises built in 1907 contain Birmingham's last remaining slipper baths. They are in need of a vastly-expensive restoration, not due to neglect but due to the use of inferior materials in their original construction.

Symphony Hall
This superb hall with its wonderful acoustics is the scene of many fine concerts by the Birmingham Symphony Orchestra and many other international artists. It is a worthy centre of culture for the second city.

Gudwara Bebe Nanakiji Temple, Rookery Road, Handsworth
To think this was the ex-Plaza ballroom, where the author saw the Bee Gees, The Kinks,
The Move and The Turtles perform live. Note how the blue in the temple matches the sky.

**Dhamma Talaka,
Birmingham Buddist Vihara,
Osier Street, Edgbaston**
Another structure which defines
the cultural and religious diversity
of Birmingham.

Botanical Gardens, Edgbaston

Trittiford Park and Lake, Yardley Wood
The Millstream Way leisure walk passes through this suburban park.

**Birmingham Eye
reflected in Hyatt Hotel**
I found more than one use
for the Hyatt Hotel's
reflective qualities.

Saracen's Head, King's Norton
Sometimes it is the part rather than the whole which serves as the best photographic composition. This ancient hostelry was once the village pub for King's Norton.

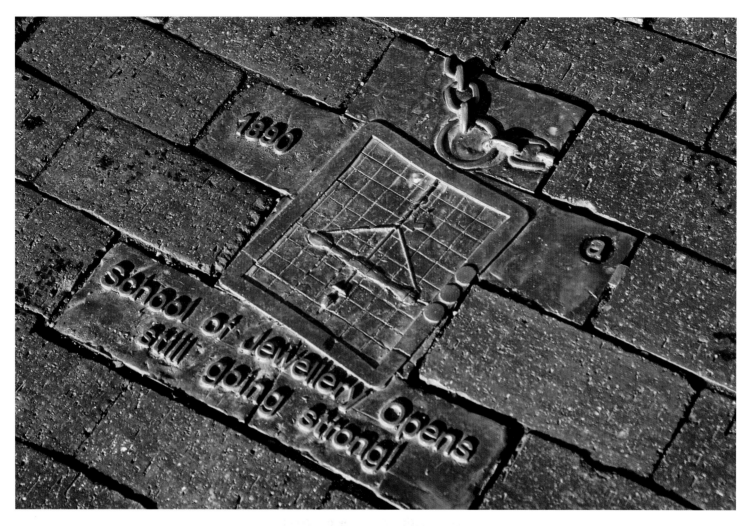

Pavement guide to the Jewellery Quarter, Hockley
Seen in Frederick Street, this is one of several paving-slab guides to this famous trading area.

Goldsmith, 26 Frederick Street
The doorway to 26 Frederick Street,
Hockley makes a statement in itself.

Clock, Vyse Street, Hockley
One of several similar clocks
found in the city. This one
commemorates the Boer War.

Clock Tower, Birmingham University, Selly Oak
Popularly known as 'Big Brum', this is a majestic landmark of the city, here seen decorated and framed with autumn foliage.

Parsons Hill canalside towpath, King's Norton
The Birmingham and Worcester Canal provides a sylvan haven.

Suburban scene, Swanshurst Lane, King's Heath
Some editing of traffic shows this suburb at its leafy best.

St Chad's Roman Catholic Cathedral
An unusual view of Birmingham's Roman Catholic cathedral.

St Philip's Cathedral
This view of the Georgian cathedral
was taken at a quiet time on a Sunday,
and gives a sense of serenity to what is
a hectic thoroughfare during the week.

O'Neill's Pub, Harborne
Formerly-named The Junction,
this popular pub is built on
the corner of two roads.

Barton's Arms, Newtown

The Barton's Arms at Newtown is one of Birmingham's most famous pubs, and a listed building. Again, note the terracotta brickwork – and the timing of the photograph with no traffic on the Walsall Road.

Winter over Rubery and Frankley Beeches, from Beacon Hill
A hoar frost and temperature inversion grips the landscape from the highest point
of the Lickey Hills. See the following picture for variation in the seasons.

Summer over Rubery and Frankley Beeches, from Beacon Hill

Moseley Bog
A lady walks her dog in this local nature reserve,
which is known to have been frequented by J.R.R. Tolkien in his youth.

Tangle, Moseley Bog
Tolkien is thought to have derived inspiration for his *Lord of the Rings* classic
from the twisted chaos of wetland vegetation that is Moseley Bog.

**Water tower,
Waterworks Road, Edgbaston**
This and the next picture of
Perrott's Folly is said to have
fired Tolkien's imagination for
The Two Towers, now a sell-out
film success.

58

**Perrott's Folly,
Waterworks Road, Edgbaston**
In fact the 'Two Towers' are at
least 200 metres apart, and
not at all related. They can be
seen as a (distant) pair from
one angle, but photographically,
are better shown separately.

59

**Lenches Trust Almshouses
and 'No 1' (office block), Five Ways**
The almshouses date from the 1830s
while the office block was built 150
years later, both buildings making
diverse design statements.

Five Ways Shopping Centre from Five Ways Island

Arcadian Centre, Hurst Street
This is a recent development near the Hippodrome.

Sunday gathering, Hurst Street
All kinds of people meet here on Sunday afternoons – and I mean ALL kinds of people!

Birmingham Repertory Theatre, Centenary Square
'The Rep' has occupied this site since the 1970s, and the architecture
fits in well with more up-to-date buildings in the vicinity.

The Mailbox
A twenty-first century development of smart shops and bars. Shown here is the facade facing the Suffolk Ringway.

Powell's Pool, Sutton Park

This and the following picture give some indication of two areas at opposite ends of the city, where escape into countryside is easily accessible for residents. Sutton Park is a 2500-acre nature reserve of ancient woodlands, medieval fishing pools and heathland, just 10 miles from the city centre.

Walking on Waseley Hills
This beautiful country park is managed, as are the Lickey Hills, by Worcestershire Countryside Services.
The beauty of the may blossom on the 'Badger Walk' is shown in this composition.

Soho House, Handsworth
The former home of pioneering engineer Matthew Boulton in Soho Avenue is now a museum.
This was the venue for meetings of the famed Lunar Society.

Millennium Point
The twenty-first century version of the former science
museum includes the 'Think Tank' among many other
exhibits related to the work of Boulton.

View opposite the National Indoor Arena
One of the popular pubs along the canal side walk, with familiar city centre buildings in the distance.

Narrow boat cruise and Sea Life Centre
The exterior of the Sea Life Centre building is functional, rather than
matching its surroundings. The boat and pedestrians add interest to the scene.

Museum and Art Gallery, Council House and Town Hall
This shot from the Adrian Boult Hall had to be compromised because of works going on in Chamberlain Square.

Town Hall
The classical neo-Roman architecture of the imposing Town Hall
is well seen from the walkway by the Adrian Boult Hall.

Summer meadow, Woodgate Valley
This largely wild country park has many delightful trails to follow. The meadow near the visitor centre
is managed in the old-fashioned way, giving rise to this riot of colourful wildflowers.

Winter, Woodgate Valley
Snow clings to the Turkey oaks on one of the wilder trails in the Woodgate Valley Country Park.

**Selfridges and the shadow of
St Martin's Church, Bull Ring**
In this picture, the ancient
parish church of Birmingham
is shadowed in the modern
shapes of the Selfridges building.

Abstract, Selfridges building
Sexy curves and silver discs
are the main features of this
compelling new building.
They are so attractive that one
of the discs was recently stolen.

77

Victoria Square
Instantly recognisable even in silhouette, Queen Victoria is enhanced
by the golden light on the Council House and the blue sky above.

River Goddess, Victoria Square
Nicknamed by Brummies as 'The Floozie in the Jacuzzi', this modern sculpture
is another focal point where people gather. Note the former head post office in
the right background, saved from demolition by the Victorian Society.

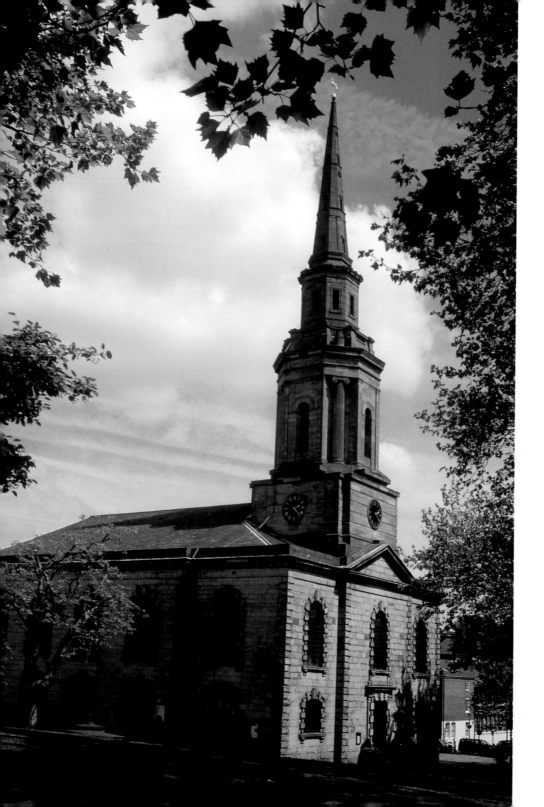

St Paul's Church, Hockley
Perfectly situated in the square
bearing its name, the church,
which dates from 1779,
is framed by sycamores.

BT Tower from Newhall Street
The highest landmark in Birmingham (500 feet), towers above the period buildings of Newhall Street.
The criss-cross jet vapours put a fascinating stamp on the picture.

Hall 5, N.E.C.
The National Exhibition Centre, adjacent to the airport, began life in the mid-1970s.

International Convention Centre
This was an early shot of the building just after its completion in the early '90s.
The 'Forward' Statue came and went through the work of arsonists.
The sign, 'Symphony Hall' has been added since over the glass frontage.

The Oratory, Edgbaston
The photograph hides unwanted subject matter beneath the Roman Catholic church, whose interior is most impressive.

Guru Nanak Nishkam Sewak Jatha (Sikh) Temple
Again, the part in the composition is preferable to the whole, as seen along Soho Road, Handsworth.

Symphony Court
Canada geese patrol even city centre waterways.

Symphony Court
This image shows how the new architecture captures the flavour of the Dutch city of Amsterdam.

National Indoor Arena and canalsides
This is the classic view seen from Broad Street.

Close-up, National Indoor Arena

Millennium Window, St Paul's Church, Hockley

A founder of Birmingham
The time-worn tomb of Sir William De Bermingham, situated inside
St Martin's-in-the-Bull-Ring Church, is Birmingham's oldest monument, dating from 1325.

Birmingham from Waseley Hills, with Frankley Beeches
The city skyline stands proud from this and several other viewpoints.
Frankley Beeches were given over to the National Trust by the Cadbury family.

Birmingham from the Pheasey Estate

Star City
Situated in The Heartlands area and served by new roads,
Star City is a typical modern shopping and leisure complex.

New Bull Ring Shopping Centre
Another view of Birmingham's latest shopping showpiece.

Old Fire Station, Legge Lane, Hockley

Windows and lamp, St Paul's Square, Hockley

King's Norton Grammar School
This fifteenth-century building is relatively small, and apparently may have once stood on stilts.

Blakesley Hall, Yardley
This fine late-sixteenth-century building is framed by diagonal struts.

Sikh and Temple
The two subjects relate, both in kind and in photographic composition.
The venue is the Guru Ravidass Bhavan Temple off Grove Lane, Handsworth.

Central Mosque, Highgate
The focal point of Islam in Birmingham, and a building not to be missed when driving on the Inner Ring Road.

Bull Ring Outdoor Market
The Rotunda and St Martin's
Church form the backdrop to this
photograph of the bustling market.
There has probably been a market
in Birmingham's Bull Ring
for at least 800 years.

Steve, Bull Ring market trader
A portrait of one of the characters of the outdoor market.

The Argent Centre, Frederick Street, Hockley
Built in 1863 for W. Wiley, a gold pen manufacturer. Note the Italianate towers
and Florentine tracery around the windows of this characterful building.

Back-to-back houses, Inge Street
Generations of Brummies were born and brought up in houses
like these. But these buildings in Inge Street are supposedly the
last of their type remaining in Birmingham. Thankfully they
are being preserved and renovated by the National Trust.

Moor Street Station
Preserved in its original Great Western Railway style, the station is still in use,
and the Great Western engine remains as a reminder of times gone by.

Inside Moor Street Station
More Great Western Railway designs seen in a different composition.

Cruise narrowboat, off Broad Street
Another canal scene tells why this
area is so popular with visitors.
With more canals than Venice,
Birmingham's canal heritage is
now seen as an important part
of the city's culture and history.

Icon Gallery, Oozells Street
This building was originally a school built in 1877, but is now a leading art gallery.
The tower is a replacement of the original.

Handsworth Park, Winter

Weeping willows, Handsworth Park

Terracotta steeples, Corporation Street
The Victoria Law Courts (left) and the Methodist Central Hall (right) are testaments to an
architectural fad of the past. 'Birmingham terracotta' was once the 'must have' for contemporary architects.

Aston Hall, Trinity Road, Aston
This fine red-brick Jacobean mansion was built between 1618-35 by Sir Thomas Holte,
after whom the famous Holte End at neighbouring Villa Park is named.

Under the A38(M), Spaghetti Junction
Somehow, oilseed rape has found a place to grow under one of Britain's busiest and most famous road junctions.

Bull Ring, interior
Mirroring the cars at Spaghetti
Junction, shoppers transport
themselves around the
Bull Ring escalators.

Edgbaston Reservoir
This early morning visit was rewarded with the boatman in situ.

Swans in flight, Edgbaston Reservoir
This was purely a grabbed shot, when instinct came in to capture the moment.

**Jeweller's frontage,
Vyse Street, Hockley**

The Hoar Stone, Hockley
This glacial erratic rests just
inside Hockley Cemetery in
Warstone Lane, which itself is a
derivation of Hoar Stone.

119

Great Western Arcade
This fine piece of high Victoriana
was an absolute must for inclusion.

120

Nechells Gas Works
These three and several more gas towers dominate the skyline in Nechells.

Show of daffodils, Woodgate Valley Country Park
The country park car park is graced by daffodils in spring.

Botanical Gardens
Another corner of the gardens, with a yucca plant in full flower.

St Augustine's Church, Edgbaston
The centrepiece of another 'swallowed' village, this fine
church and spire are now found in a tranquil urban suburb.

St Laurence's Church, Northfield
This thirteenth to fourteenth century church, once another village centre, contains some Norman work, but is mainly in the Early English style. Nearby is the Great Stone Inn and adjoining village pound, where stray animals were once impounded.

Gas Street Basin
There is always interest in canal boats, and certainly so here.

**Architectural contrast 2,
Gas Street Basin**
The hostelry, with customers
in the foreground, is set against
the facade of the Hyatt Hotel.

Selly Manor, Bournville
This manor house dating from the fifteenth century was moved to this site by George Cadbury in 1912-16.

Close-up, Old Crown, Deritend
This is the oldest pub in the city, and was recently sympathetically restored.

**Nelson Statue
and St Martin's, Bull Ring**
The victor of Trafalgar is celebrated
in this fine statue in the Bull Ring.

**Christmas shoppers
and St Martin's, Bull Ring**

131

Visitor centre, Bournville Village Green
Visitors can take the tour around Chocolate World from this centre in
the heart of the Cadbury's model village Bournville estate.

Bournville Junior School
The school has a unique Carillon bell tower, seen here.

Bulls Head and Morris Minor, King's Norton
I just couldn't pass up this little cameo!

Warwickshire County Cricket Ground, Edgbaston
Warwickshire are pictured bowling out Surrey in a game they comfortably won at one of the
premier grounds of English cricket, and the scene of many a memorable Test match.

On the wall no. 1
The photograph in the Charles Road Recreation Ground at Small Heath was set up.
I asked the kids to sit with legs dangling over the grafitti-adorned wall, with hands on knees.
That's how I saw it, anyway.

On the wall no. 2
This shows how a photographer can develop a theme. A competition judge had admired the
previous image, but mentioned that he would have liked to see a figure at the bottom of the picture.
I went back a year later on the off-chance – and this was the satisfying result.

Corner of Birmingham Institute of Art and Design (U.C.E.)
The lamp standards and façade were condensed
into the composition.

Hall of Memory and Birmingham Eye
The domed octagonal building, completed in 1924, includes one of the bronze statues
by Albert Toft – in strange contrast to the Birmingham Eye.

Bartley Green Reservoir
Much of Birmingham's water supply is piped here from the Elan Valley in central Wales.

Hay Barn Recreation Ground
This large green swathe splits apart
the urban sprawl in Hay Mills, with
the River Cole running through it.
The distant houses give scale.

141

The Rotunda

The iconic survivor of the previous Bull Ring, the famous circular tower (271 feet high) is to be refurbished. There is talk of having a revolving restaurant on top. It would certainly give a fine view of the city.

A corner of Chinatown
This is a corner of the area around Hurst Street
which is dominated by oriental restaurants and takeaways.

Pagoda and Sentinel
Holloway Circus shows the curious juxtaposition of the decorative pagoda against the very tall tower block, one of a pair on opposite sides of the road.

144